Pearson Baccalaureate PYP Readers

On Journeys

Mandy Ross

Pearson Education Limited is a company incorporated in England and Wales, having its registered office at Edinburgh Gate, Harlow, Essex, CM20 2JE. Registered company number: 872828

www.pearsonglobalschools.com

© Pearson Education Ltd 2009.

Designed by Celia Floyd

ISBN 978 0 435995 83 6

20 19 18
IMP 10 9 8 7 6

Printed in China (CTPSC/06)

British Library Cataloguing in Publication Data
A full catalogue record for this book is available from the British Library.

Acknowledgements
Quotation on page 19 from 'Birmingham Voices' by Helen Lloyd and Lucy Harland, Tempus Publishing and BBC Radio WM 'The Century Speaks', 1999. The Publishers would like to thank the following for permission to reproduce photographs:
Camera Press: 26; Corbis/ Ecoscene: 22, 28; Hulton Archive: 8, 9, 13, 17, 18; Popperfoto: 11, 21, 24, 27; Quadrant: 14; Ross and Parry: 29; Topham: 4, 7, 10, 12, 15, 19, 20, 23, 25; TRIP/Helene Rogers: 5; Victoria and Albert Museum: 6, 16.

Our thanks to Stuart Copeman for his help in the preparation of this book.

Contents

Words printed in **bold letters like these** are explained in the Glossary.

Each **decade** is highlighted on a timeline at the bottom of the page.

Then and now

How many different ways have you travelled? In 1900, people could travel by horse, bicycle, boat, steam train or on foot.

In the early 1900s, some people never left the area where they were born the whole of their lives. Others travelled great distances across the world. Many never saw their family and friends again.

In the 1900s horse-drawn carriages and buses were common ways of travelling.

Traffic jams often bring our cities and motorways to a standstill.

Since 1900, new **vehicles** have changed our journeys around the Earth – and even beyond, into Space. Ordinary people, not just the very rich, can buy a car or fly in aeroplanes. We can travel further and faster than ever before. But there are new problems too, such as traffic jams and air **pollution**.

1900s: Journeys

How do you travel to school or to the shops? At the start of the 20th century, most people made local journeys on foot. Many children walked up to three or four miles each way to school, especially if they lived in the countryside.

Some people were too poor to buy shoes, so the children had to walk barefoot.

The first aeroplanes started taking off in the early 1900s. They could fly only short distances. In 1909, Frenchman Louis Blériot was the first person to fly from France to England.

A French girl who watched the take-off remembers:
'When we knew that Blériot was going to leave, all the children in the district gathered in a field. Everyone clapped and waved, everyone shouted 'Bravo!'... There was immense joy when we heard he'd landed on the cliffs of Dover.'

1910s: Steam trains

If people were going on a long journey, they would often go by steam train. These trains went more slowly than our trains today.

On Bank Holidays families went on day-trips and outings. Many people went by steam train to the seaside for the day. There were fairs, sporting events, and brass bands playing in public parks.

People often travelled to the seaside by steam train.

Trains played an important part in the **First World War**. Many soldiers travelled to the battlefields by steam train. They were waved off by tearful women and children. Hospital trains carried wounded soldiers back from the battlefields to safety and medical care.

Soldiers travelled to war on steam trains.

1920s: Long distance journeys

Many British people wanted to make a new life in Australia. In the 1920s, over 200,000 British people set off. The journey by steamship took six weeks. People slept in small cabins and ate in shared dining rooms. Many people made lifelong friendships on the trip.

This family were going by steamship to Australia in 1922.

Motor vehicles

Only richer people could afford to buy a car. Other people went on motor buses, which went faster than the old horse-drawn buses and trams. Motor coaches called charabancs took people on outings. New motor lorries were in use although trains still carried goods over long distances.

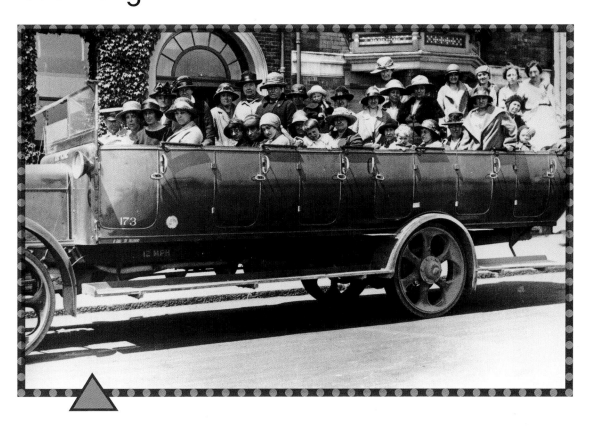

Women on a charabanc outing in 1928.

1930s: On the move

Journeys called **protest** marches are organized when people want to show that they are angry about something. Have you ever seen a protest march?

In Jarrow, in north east England, thousands of men had lost their jobs building ships. Their families grew poor and hungry. In 1936, about 200 men from Jarrow walked 440km to London on a protest march.

The Jarrow marchers' long journey showed the **government** how angry they were.

In 1938, just before the **Second World War**, many German and Austrian Jewish children escaped to Britain as **refugees**. They travelled on the Kindertransport, or children's trains.

A Jewish refugee remembers:

'Just before we came to the border, the Germans entered the carriage, and said 'You think you will get away, but we'll catch you yet!' Everybody started crying. When the train left Germany, we cheered…'

Jewish refugee children arriving to safety in England on the Kindertransport.

1940s: To war – and back

Have you ever flown in an aeroplane? In the 1940s, ordinary people could never expect to travel in an aeroplane.

During the **Second World War**, bomber planes flew across Europe on deadly air raids. They dropped bombs in enemy towns and cities.

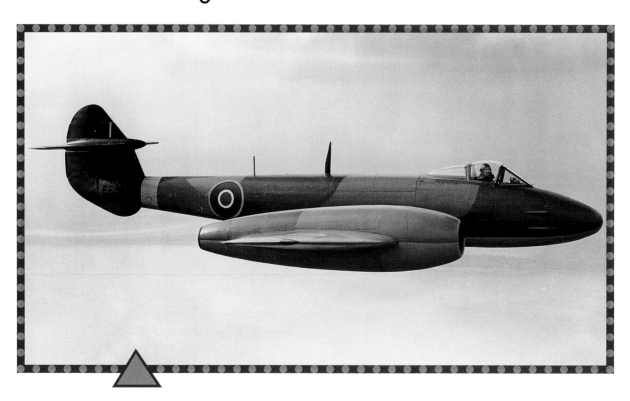

New high-speed jet planes, like the Gloster Meteor, began to be used as fighters.

Small fishing boats helped to rescue soldiers from Dunkirk.

In May 1940, 338,000 British and French soldiers were stranded on the beaches at Dunkirk, in northern France. They needed to escape from the German Army. Hundreds of small fishing boats sailed from England and helped the Royal Navy to rescue all the soldiers.

1940s and 1950s: Coming to Britain

After the war, the British **government** encouraged people from countries such as India, Pakistan and the West Indies to come to fill empty jobs in Britain. The journey by steamship took two to three weeks, or even longer.

Many immigrants brought just one or two suitcases. What would you take if you were moving to a new country?

Arriving in 1948 on the Empire Windrush, the first ship to arrive from Jamaica.

A **passenger** on one of the first ships from Jamaica remembers:

'I wanted to see the country that influenced my education. Most of us were young men who came over on a wave of excitement to try life in a new country.'

Many black and Asian people who arrived in Britain were able to build a good new life. But others met with **discrimination** because of their race.

Many immigrants found work in London, like this bus conductor.

1950s: Leisure trips

In the 1950s people were keen to get back to a normal life after the war. Going on holidays and day-trips was popular. Where would you choose to go for a day-trip or a holiday?

Hiking was a favourite weekend pastime. Many people caught a bus or train into the countryside, and spent the day walking on footpaths through the hills and fields.

TOM PURVIS

EAST COAST
By London & North Eastern Railway

This advert encouraged people to take the train to the countryside for a weekend away.

More people owned motor cars, so they could drive wherever they wanted to go.

Most people stayed in Britain for their holidays and visited the seaside. A man called Billy Butlin set up his Butlins holiday camps at seaside resorts all around Britain. Other families stayed in boarding houses, where the landlady cooked all their meals.

1960s: High speeds

During the 1960s, the first motorways were built in Britain to allow people to drive at higher speeds. Have you ever travelled on a motorway?

More people were buying and driving cars. A new small car called the Mini went on sale in the 1960s. It was affordable, trendy, and very popular.

A competition to see how many people could fit into a Mini.

In the 1960s, American and Soviet scientists were developing space travel. Both countries wanted to be the first to send people into space.

Yuri Gagarin, a Soviet, was the first person in space in 1961. But in 1969, Neil Armstrong, an American, was the first man on the Moon.

Millions of people watched on television as Neil Armstrong stepped onto the Moon.

1970s: New ways of getting about

In 1973, the cost of oil rose steeply, and there were shortages of petrol. Car owners had to share their car journeys, or travel by **public transport**.

By the 1970s, new hovercraft were being used for short journeys across the sea such as from England to France. Hovercraft can go faster than ferries, hovering above the water's surface.

A hovercraft is a kind of boat that can carry passengers on short journeys.

In 1976, Concorde became the first jet plane to fly **passengers** faster than the speed of sound. It could fly from London to New York and back again in less than a day. A normal aeroplane would take about 7 hours to fly just one way. Flying on Concorde was too expensive for most people.

Concorde was the quickest way for passengers to travel in the 1970s.

1980s: By air and sea

Have you ever been on holiday to another country? By the 1980s, the cost of air travel and holidays abroad was falling. Many more people could afford to take holidays in other countries. In 1986, 22 million British people went to another country for their holidays. In 1957, only 2 million had done so.

Lots of families now travelled abroad for their holidays.

1900   1910   1920   1930   1940

In the 1980s, many people from Vietnam, in south east Asia, wanted to leave their country after a long and fierce war. Thousands of people tried to escape by sea to neighbouring countries, often in tiny, overcrowded boats.

It was a dangerous journey. Many of the Boat People, as they became known, drowned on the way. Some who survived came to live in Britain.

These Vietnamese Boat People crowded into small boats to escape the poverty and danger in Vietnam.

1990s: Freedom to travel?

By the 1990s, **public transport** was not running smoothly. Tickets grew more expensive but train and bus services became unreliable. People without cars had more problems getting about especially if they lived in the countryside.

In the meantime, more cars and lorries made the roads very crowded. By 1999 there was almost one car for every two people in Britain.

*The **Channel Tunnel** opened in 1994, making the journey from England to France much quicker.*

1930   1940

Refugees travelling out of Kosovo, southern Europe, on tractors, the only transport they could get.

Refugees

In the 1990s, the number of **refugees** rose around the world. Most refugees escape to nearby countries, so that they can go home when it is safe again. Some refugees come to Britain to live in safety.

2000s: Journeys today

All over the world, people are using cars and aeroplanes more and more. This means that we are quickly using up the Earth's supplies of fuels, such as coal, oil and gas, and creating **pollution**. Car makers are trying to design cars which run on cleaner, **renewable fuels**.

This car is powered by the Sun rather than petrol.

A 'walking bus' – adults walk children to school in a group, reducing the number of car journeys needed.

Many local **councils** are introducing bus and bike lanes in towns and cities. These encourage people to walk, cycle and use **public transport** instead of using their cars.

If we don't act quickly, journeys in the 21st century may have to become more like those in the 19th century – before cars and planes were invented.

Find out for yourself

You could talk to people you know in your neighbourhood. Ask them about their journeys to school, to work or on holiday, and how these journeys have changed through their lifetime. Ask them if they have made other journeys, for instance moving from one country to another.

You could also ask if they have any old photographs of journeys they made when they were younger.

Books

Linkers: Journeys, A & C Black, 1996
Transport Around the World: Cars, Boats and Ships, Trains, Planes, Heinemann Library, 2000

Glossary

Channel Tunnel a long tunnel built under the water between England and France

council a group of people elected to decide how to run local services

discrimination when someone is treated differently or badly, for example, because of their race or sex

First World War when some countries, including Britain, were at war with Germany, 1914-1918

government a group of people elected to run the country

passenger someone who rides in a vehicle

pollution when dirt or waste makes the environment unclean

protest when people want to show that they are angry about something

public transport vehicles, such as trains, buses or trams, which anyone can travel on

refugee people who have had to leave their own country because of war, hunger or cruel governments to find safety elsewhere

renewable fuel fuel that will not run out, such as solar power (from the Sun) or wind power

Second World War when some countries, including Britain, were at war with Germany, 1939-1946

vehicle something that moves or carries things, for instance a car, lorry or train

Index